Sitting on the Sidelines is one poet's rally cry to a stony-raced world, a calling to honour the heart; to live from the heart without shame. Punctuated with the apt words of writers both contemporary and historic, it is uniquely presented and complied. Each poem is staccato, to-the-point yet melodic, piercing, and the reader needn't strain their imagination to visualise these pieces being performed on stage, effortlessly embodied as spoken word. With themes spanning love, pain, and Okor's experience as a black man of Nigerian origin living in London, *Sitting on the Sidelines* is as topically diverse as it is refreshing.
– Carys Maloney, author of *Letters from the Barrier*

Mase Okor's *Sitting on the Sidelines* delivers a delicate balance of sophistication, charm and vulnerability. Okor's use of language and vernacular unravels somewhat like a symphonic movement, transporting you with rhythmic variety through moments of joyful exuberance to moments of fearless introspection. *Sitting on the Sidelines* is both informative and enormously insightful, but above all, exists as a manifesto of empowerment. A work to be treasured and cherished at all costs.
– Durone Stokes, actor

Mase Okor's *Sitting on the Sidelines* is a piercing debut collection trying to make sense of the world and going beyond dualities in its effort to explore what it feels like being a young black man and an artist today. Dualism and the complexity of it are at the heart of the collection. Starting with the image of the two faces of Janus, Mase Okor moves effortlessly from the classic to the contemporary. With the use of quotes (from popular culture and science to music and poetry) and the power of the dictionary as starting points, we're guided through trauma and hope, self-doubt and self-love, black identity and black masculinity.
The title poem – 'Sitting On The Sidelines (S.O.S.)' – works as a bridge bringing these two sides of Mase as a poet to face each other, and encapsulates the soul of the collection. Here, pain and numbness go hand in hand and one can almost taste the hurt, the bitter self-doubt of not being enough, the never-ending sense that pain is here to stay. And yet, within all that, there appear the 'sidelines' which Mase sees as pit stops and birthplaces of rejuvenation. 'Janus pt 2', the final poem, goes even further and in a perfect circle the collection's two faces collide to create a gateway to translucent hope. *Sitting on the Sidelines* is a wonderfully engaging collection, enveloped in a fearless desire to be true to itself. Mase Okor is a promising young poet and definitely one to watch!
– Katerina Kolouri, poet and translator

Sitting on the Sidelines is ambitious debut collection that is looking everywhere under the sun to make sense of the world today and Mase Okor wildly succeeds. The poems position themselves conversation with popular culture and critical theory in order to mirror the lived experience of a young artist. The poet's voice emerges in the selection of quotes he chooses to respond to here; the range is exquisite from bell hooks to V.S. Ramachandran and more. There is a serious desire to engage with everything the world has to offer this young Black-British author. Look out for everything Mase Okor does!
– Julia Rose Lewis, author of *Misuse*

Mase Okor invokes an intimacy, expression and power that not only carves vivid images and depictions, but I would dare say will make you break a little bit from inside, particularly as a male. There is a raw emotion and feeling in the text that is both refreshing and which you can identify with. Its style not just its message embodies redefining masculinity.
– Jerome Sewell, Managing director Therapeutic productions CIC and Unique Talent CIC

Mase Okor

Sitting on
the Sidelines

About the author

Mase Okor is a Black-British performer and poet of Nigerian origin and was born in 1999, in South-East London where he still lives and works. He studied Drama and English Literature at the University of Greenwich. He has taken part in storytelling workshops to hone his craft and acting skills. He worked as an assistant director for a short film titled *Brother's Keeper*, which explores black single-parent households, brotherhood and family.

Mase's work focuses primarily on gender and race, specifically masculinity and black identity. He explores these themes through the mediums of music, dance and poetry to engage with his audience on an intellectual and intimate level. His inspirations draw heavily from posthumous and contemporary black artists and creators such as: James Baldwin, Chinua Achebe, a Nigerian Nobel-prize winning novelist, Tristan Fynn-Aiduenu, a British-Ghanaian theatre-maker who co-directed *For Black Boys Have Considered Suicide When the Hue Gets Too Heavy* (2021), and Caleb Femi, a British Nigerian poet who wrote the critically acclaimed poem collection *Poor* (2020).

Mase's music inspirations range from Nigerian multi-instrumentalist and Afrobeat pioneer Fela Kuti to Compton-born rapper and Pulitzer Prize winner Kendrick Lamar. In using music to perform, Mase blends these genres with the consciousness of race, identity and masculinity to further educate his audience.

SITTING ON THE SIDELINES
FIRST EDITION, 2024
Sitting on the Sidelines copyright © MASE OKOR

*Printed by Femmesocial Press as a limited edition
of 200 copies.*

ISBN: 978-1-0687480-0-4

Femmesocial Press, 2024.

*Designed and typeset by Vendula Markova
Cover design by Ema Cegledyova
Edited by Petra Palkovacsova
Photography by Lou Smith*

Printed in the Czech Republic.

To the boundless black boys redefining masculinity.

Above all else, guard your heart, for everything you do
flows from it.
✳ *Proverbs 4:23*

To the young kings, lean into your vulnerability and
re-define masculinity, lead with heart. There's so many
different ways to be brilliant, I believe you and every
human being is born with a masterful gift.
✳ *Beyoncé*

I. ORIGIN

noun /ˈɒrɪdʒ(ɪ)n/

The point or place where
something begins, arises,
or is derived.

JÅNUS pt. 1

The genesis of empty promises can leave you full of degradation and delusions.
The lavish gateway of lascivious lies, lie inside those who are sly like the hiss of a venomous tongue which flicks at nightfall amongst the dew of oblivious hazy pastures.

Back   and   forth.

Trauma is a funny thing, like seeing a particular/familiar stranger multiple times in different locations.

Strange   yet   familiar.

We think in dichotomies and dualities thinking it's all– ...

This   or   that.

When in reality life is a plethora of complexities, you, two-faced and simultaneously one-sided like a paradoxical coin, until all that was left in the pockets of my heart was zero-tolerance.

I, too fazed by what was real and what potentially could have been.

Us, two faces meet, collide, then part like...

Night   and   day.

Back   to   back.

Past   and   future.

Like the two faces of JÅNUS.
Dawn
  Birth
    Rise
     Unfold
       Debut
         Begins with you.

II. AMBIVALENT

adjective /amˈbɪvələnt/

Having mixed feelings or
contradictory ideas about
something or someone.

We are all fools in love.
  ✳ *Jane Austen*

Why don't I love you?

When you put two and two together, two hearts, two stories, two eyes which see the window to my soul. It should make sense.

Curtains that uncover pure kindness that lets the light in. It shines across me like the start of spring. I thought you and I would be a special thing.

Why don't I love you?

The soothing flames of your fireplace fill me with bliss. You make me feel safe, but the fervent glow is dimming. Discomfort clenches me in the reclining sofa of what should be ease. Interest declines.

The house in which we make home has degraded into a trap, illicit, complicit, surely this can't be it?

The honeymoon drug has become fruitless and unsweet. The side effects of confusion fog my mind. Withdrawal is like a mindless thought left behind. The passion fades but you are still nice.

But nice just isn't nice enough. The poignancy permeates my mind and pierces my heart, peeling layers upon layers of precious love to give.

So why don't I love you?

There is no love without a little bit of madness.
✳ Friedrich Nietzsche

Limerence

or li·mer·ance

/ ˈlɪ mɛr əns /

the state of being obsessively infatuated with someone, usually accompanied by delusions of or a desire for an intense romantic relationship with that person.

Limerence got a lick on me, a kick on me, one deep look and then you'll see.

In sun filled gardens, rose-tinted glasses see what's not real, perhaps it's me that's the spectacle?

It picked on me, fixed onto me, unexpectantly, on my mind, dusk till dawn. I sigh, I fawn.

Is it love and romance or just hazy limerence?

You need me, trust me you'll see.

Brown-skinned, sweet like honey baby. Lips like peaches, sweet but sparing.

Addicted to your taste, but was it all a waste?

Inkling/run dry

We were eternal, fraternal your touch as warm as a thermal on a dewy winter's morning dipped in grey. We drew on each other like journals revealing our deepest internal monologues.

Then I had an inkling something was sinking, had me thinking we were bonded together, sealed, healed, so why do I yield for you?

I penned all my love for you, maybe that's why the ink for myself has run dry.

Don't get green skin (green skin), keep contact (keep contact)
Don't say goodbye, smell you later
✳ Tyler The Creator

---

last night in cable carts

Your cheekbones frame the curvatures of a kind face.
The portrait of pure art.
Hair laid, neat and defined in

interwoven patterns of symmetrical gymnastics.
Crescent eyes, dark, slanted, searing.
Daydreaming in the beautiful midnight of your serene sights.
Your sweet ample lips flow into mine, as we exchange long-awaited
uncharted whispers in between.
The cable cart heightens above buildings and our head above clouds
time slows as we glide seamlessly through the obsidian night sky.

Your melodious tone pours into my soul seamlessly
like the tides below us.

---

*If you are silent about your pain, they'll kill you and say
you enjoyed it.*
* *Zora Neale Hurston*

III. RESENTMENT
noun /rɪˈzɛntm(ə)nt/

Bitter indignation at having
been treated unfairly.

I'm for truth, no matter who tells it. I'm for justice, no matter who it is for or against. I'm a human being, first and foremost, and as such I'm for whoever and whatever benefits humanity as a whole.
✳ Malcolm X

Say my name

I spit my pain into rhythm. My name is a rich heavenly hymn,
bastardised like sin, but the real love starts from within.

To the boys with names with syllables that orchestrate melodies
on your lips, bouncing of the walls, ricochet through the halls,
going back and forth. Always right their wrongs when they
mispronounce, misname and mistake you.

To the girls whose names announce their royalty before they
have arrived at their throne.
The girls with the prettiest, pedantic, precious names.

Hold your sceptre and your crown high,
don't slip, don't trip, you are it girl.
Hear ye, hear ye, let them hear you.

Every time they disrespect you it mirrors their ugly disposition,
cracking and shattering their esteem. Your last name is the
heirloom of the ancestors persevering through title and spirit.
Be loud, be proud, be brave, be heard. Your names are a long
tapestry of resilience, strength, beauty and love.

Children have never been very good at listening to their elders, but they have never failed to imitate them.
∗ James Baldwin

Love's gonna get you killed.
But pride's gonna be the death of
you, and you and me
And you, and you, and you and me
And you, and you, and you and me
And you, and you, and—
∗ Kendrick Lamar

Pride is killing us

Your ego stains the growing pains of all your descendants.
In this high road called life where you can be honest and true you'd
rather sneak through the easy streets of lies and deceits.

A sleazy parlour of gambling self-respect and self-conceit.
A balancing act on the tightrope of manhood.

The truth will be uncovered when it's all too late, revealing a swirling
cocktail of toxicity: the contents of repressed tears, cloudy unsaid
thoughts and venomous drops of the sharpest serpent fang, which
lace the concoction of the downfall of man.

Soulless, apathetic, so pathetic, your pride doesn't only affect you,
your pride is killing us.

The practice of love offers no place of safety. We risk loss, hurt, pain. We risk being acted upon by forces outside our control.
✳ *bell hooks,* All About Love: New Visions

Love on E

I gave you nothing but love. Maybe that's why I haven't got none for myself.

*Being a Nigerian is abysmally frustrating
and ubelievably exciting*
* Chinua Achebe

Crazy things are happening
* Tems

*The most authentic thing about us is our capacity to create,
to overcome, to endure, to transform, to love and be greater
than our suffering*
* Ben Okri

Nigerians, we're everywhere!

Conceived in Pangea.
Shipped from the motherland.
Manufactured in the intersections of South-East London.
Dispersed all around the globe.
But nowhere near or there to call home.

Globetrotting in the NBA.
Blasting beats in the wickedest of raves.
Stunting on runways and catwalks.
Crafting infrastructures boldly.

Breaking barriers for the next generation.
We are the manifestation of our creator's elation

The Africans Giants!
      Super Eagles!
Nollywood!
        Lasgidi!
Benin City!
But it isn't all that pretty.
Things fall apart when the foundation is shifty...

Yahoo boys.
419 scammers.
Corrupt politicians.
Insane decisions.
End SARS and battle scars.
Plantain and Jollof Rice.
Afrobeat's but there's blood on the streets?

Although there's corruption and disruption in a place many calls
home.

We're all one in the same, just a different time zone.
We're here, we're there
Nigerians, we're everywhere.

IV. AMYGDALA
noun /əˈmɪgdələ/

A roughly almond-shaped
mass of grey matter inside each
cerebral hemisphere, involved
with the experiencing of
emotions.

Some people turn sad awfully young. No special reason, it seems, but they seem almost to be born that way. They bruise easier, tire faster, cry quicker, remember longer and, as I say, get sadder younger than anyone else in the world. I know, for I'm one of them.
✴ Ray Bradbury, Dandelion Wine

A Mask won't hide who you are inside
✴ Kendrick Lamar

0 fucks given

4,303 a year,

1 Every 2

Hours.

12 every day

95 times   A Week.

1 in   5 ideations,

in   14 actions,

1 in   15 attempts,

0 fucks given.

https://www.samaritans.org/about-samaritans/research-policy/suicide-facts-and-figures/latest-suicide-data/

Your pain is the breaking of the shell that encloses your understanding. It is the bitter poison by which the physician within you heals your sick self. Therefore, trust the physician and drink his remedy in silence and tranquillity.
✳ Khalil Gibran

Running around, catching a lot of light.
In the moonlight, black boys look blue.
You blue, that's what I'm gonna call you: Blue.
✳ Juan, Moonlight

A Case of the Black Boy Blues

Patient name: Creative Soul
Date: Today
Diagnosis: The Black Boy Blues

Symptoms:

> A numbness to positive emotions
> Dark skin, the darker skin tones the more severe
> Comparison to other black students who do not share
  a resemblance other than skin tone
> An inability to cry
> Frequent aches of paranoia
> Low self-esteem
> Suicidal thoughts
> An itch for a better life
> A dichotomy of rage and chronic emptiness
> Invisibility
> Irreverent responses from family and friends

Treatment:

>   1. Gratitude Tablets
>   • Begin each morning with 20 things to be grateful about.
>   Allow yourself to feel.
>   • Do not compare their social media highlight reel with
>   your real-life blooper reel.
>   • When faced with difficulty find the positives, this lesson
>   will help you to heal.
>
>   2. Laughter Syrup
>   • Spend each day watching 20 minutes of an entertaining
>   sitcom comedy.

- Do not take things so personally, laugh at the smallest of things, evolve from animosity.
- Watch a stand-comedy routine to add to the remedy.

3.Connection Capsules
- Spend 30 minutes a day conversing with a trusted friend or family member.
- Phone a friend you have not spoken to a while, any gender.
- Join a club which specialises in one of your interests, i.e. (sports, music, gaming or art). Don't surrender.

4.Nature and Exercise
- Stroll in nature more, scroll on your phone less.
- Exercise 1 hour a day (walking, cardio or bench press)
- Adequate sleep equals a decrease in stress.

5. Artistic Expression
- Spend 1 hour a day engaging in a creative task such as writing, dancing or art.
- Listen to music with messages of self-love, it is good for your heart.
- Buy something the 8-year-old you loved and allow the creativity and nostalgia to start.

6. Mindfulness Composure Therapy
- Spend 15 minutes doing meditation and breathing exercises in the morning and night again.
- Acknowledge your feelings and allow yourself to feel but not sink into them.
- Take each day step by step. Patience is key. You are a gem.

Refills: whenever necessary.

Side effects: Following instructions is proven to increase happiness, boost creativity and overall quality of life.

Notes: The Black Boy Blues is the valley of the shadow of death masked as a rite of passage. It can often be in the little things that make everything worthwhile. Be kind to yourself. Comparison is not only the thief of joy but a magnet of negativity and misfortune.

Signature:

Dr Post

We can now say with confidence that the brain is an extraordinarily plastic biological system that is in a state of dynamic equilibrium with the external world. Even its basic connections are being constantly updated in response to changing sensory demands.

  ✳ *V. S. Ramachandran*

V. MELANCHOLIA

noun /mel-ən-ˈkō-lē-ə/

Severe depression
characterized especially by
profound sadness and despair.

---

*What happened to the Motherland? They don't want to see
blacks the same as another man.*
✳ *Swiss*

*The pain I feel now is the happiness I had before.
That's the deal.*
✳ *C. S. Lewis*

Little Black King

Little Black Boys with Big Sharp Knives.
Moving in the dead of night, just trying to survive. Mean
muggin', frowning, staring and glaring.
Hiding their emotions through cussing and swearing.
Concealed tears that hide in the shadows of repression.

Little Black King, your voice is your greatest weapon. Our
history predates slavery, there's freedom in self-expression.
Achebe, Basquiat, Baldwin, Hughes.
R&B, Rock n' Roll, Gospel, the Blues.
These are the effortless talents that make you, you.

Likkle Black Yutes, you've got too much to lose.
Ducking down opps in estates of abuse.
Machetes and madness swinging in the air.
They stop, search and kill and nobody even cares.
We're not outnumbered, we're underprepared.
Little Black Brothers you need to love one another.
When will you discover that the world needs our colour!

These pigs cut deep, they oink, squeal and shoot.
The trees of South-East London bearing strange fruit.
The blood of children soiled in these streets.
Mothers burying their sons, and the cycle repeats.

A child who is not embraced by the village will burn it down to feel
warmth. The blacker the berry, the sweeter the juice.
And the darker the hue, the worse the abuse...

The price one pays for pursuing any profession or calling
is an intimate knowledge of its ugly side.
✴ _James Baldwin_

I've always had to rely on the kindness of strangers.
✴ _Blanche Dubois_, A Streetcar Named Desire

Napoleonic Code/ Under the lampshade

What's mine is yours.
What's yours is yours.
What's mine isn't even mine no more.

My heart cowers in creeks which once bloomed across valleys.

In my home, the intricate Japanese lampshade hangs among a moth-
like bulb that provides protection. The cosmic band-aid for my soul.
But you ripped it off when I least expected. And sent me into
a black hole spiralling.

Under the lampshade anything goes.
Under the lampshade friends turn to foes.
Under the lampshade everything is exposed.

In the dark there's no shadows, demons aren't demons, and believers
and heathens are fraternal twins.
Salt tastes like sugar cubes.
And the lies dissolve sweeter than the truth.

The burning house of my heart is endangered.
For someone I thought was real, turned out to be much stranger.

Uninvited, unrequited, enveloped in my space. What appears as
a gift on the outside but something much sinister within...

Soiled wooden floorboards, rusty brass horns echo through the
hallways, hypnotic squeals of the Varsouviana polka blares and
shrieks, staining the blemished walls. Creasing and crunching,
constricting my heart flow, cramping my lungs and crushing my
soul.

Cracks creak and cut into discoloured windows, paint chips away
and peels revealing the musings of the teardrops of youth.

A mosaic of neglected black boyhood.

A purple light glows within the confines of these fractured walls.
Illuminating the duality of innocence and trauma as they collide
into one singular entity.

I should've listened to my intuition.
The pain of my regret can't compare.
But anything can happen under the lampshade.

I had once believed strangers would rely on the kindness of me, now
I rely on the kindness of strangers.

———————

Ease is a greater threat to progress than hardship.
✳ *Denzel Washington*

You must believe in yourself; you must really get up off of the sidelines of your own life and get in there and fight for you. You are the best person out there to put up the good fight for you.
✳ *Sheryl Lee Ralph*

———————

Sitting On The Sidelines (S.O.S.)

On the precipice of pain and bliss
there is blame and an abyss.

I am
sitting on the sidelines.

Idle.
Waiting.
Longing.
Frustrating.
Destroying.
Annoying.

An abscess filled of misery develops inside.
Does this aching pain ever subside?

I'm hurting.
Shrinking on the sidelines, sinking in the sidelines, screaming for
help and I'm slipping in the blind sides.

Always giving, nurturing, healing others. Pouring out my nutrients
to bloom your garden. Meanwhile, mine becomes a cemetery of
broken dreams, skulls cracked with soiled seams.

How do I just let go?

How am I numb but in excruciating pain at the same time?
Don't say you love me when I'm gone.

My best just wasn't enough.

My pain is a testament to the depth of my love. The receipt, proof of purchase that I bought into love. No refunds, just memories exchanged for time and energy.

My feelings sway in murky seas singing the minstrels of the bluest song. I call out my distress signal, my cry from the heart. Deserted, an outcast castaway surrounded by ravenous waters and unrelenting thoughts.

Friends become drinking buddies.
Birthdays become reminders.
Potential lovers transpire into flings.
Bed rotting looks like peace.
People simply fade away.
There tends to be nothing more to say.
My mind is bound to decay.

So sad how things turn sour.
Stood by you in your lonely hour.
I feel weaker.
At times it is bleaker.
It gets harder.
But you get stronger.

Then it gets clear.
Less fear.
You persevere.
You fight with might.
You pray the pain away.
And to all dismay.
Things divinely fall into place.
Sidelines are the pit stops we rejuvenate ourselves in, where we fall

and breakdown so we can breakthrough the glass ceilings of repression and break the mould society bounds us boundless black boys too. Where we rest but never lay down for too long.

For it catapults us into the frontlines convulsing our poignant pain into profound power.

I'm too much of an erratic, moody baby! I don't have the passion anymore, and so remember, it's better to burn out than to fade away.
✳ Kurt Cobain

Burn Out/ Fade Away

Burnouts and fade aways.
Nightmares and brighter days.
How do I lock in and not stray away?
Seeking Nirvana when there's hell to pay.

Pain pangs through to the lips of liars.
I persist over and over till the self-doubt transpires.
When the dream is within reach, I feel weak.
They feign kindness but hide behind their malice mystique.

The tides fade and flow across the sands of time.
I realise my gifts and the job that I have been assigned.
Talent and flair, countless years of arduous work. Trials
and errors, 'friends' sneak like snakes and lurk.

When the party inevitably concludes.
What is left in this drowning interlude?
Engulfing tomorrow's hopes and dreams.
Some things are not ever what they seem.

It is hard to be happy when your heart is on fire.
But the joy of what I love fuels all my deepest desires.
Kaluuya, Boyega, Idris, Imhangbe, Ward. Acting,
directing, writing, why can't I have it all?

It's in the early mornings and restless nights.
The endless rehearsals and trying to get it just right.
Through spiteful lows, no shows, sorrows and many noes.
All the fruits of my labour will become a banquet to be bestowed.

No matter what happens, or how bad it seems today, life does go on, and it will be better tomorrow.
* *Maya Angelou*

I'll tell you what Freedom is to me. No fear.
* *Nina Simone*

Freedom

Cut me loose from the pain, the tears and disdain.
The trauma that seeps in when the world sleeps in.
I stand on the edge of sleepless nights and not a care in sight.

Yet, in my darkest hour there's you.
You have always been around. When I was lost, it was you I found.
When I'm drowning in the depths of all those who left and laughed.
It was you who caught me and placed me in your life raft.

Resuscitated the lost soul, buried in repression.
You are me: the broken reflection. The cracks
and scars that was once concealed is a road to freedom
and being healed.

Self-love is the foundation of our loving practice. Without it our other efforts to love fail. Giving ourselves love we provide our inner being with the opportunity to have the unconditional love we may have always longed to receive from someone else.
* *bell hooks,* All About Love: New Visions

VI. PHILAUTIA
noun /Φιλαυτία/

Self-love.

The Makings of You

Out with the old view.
And in with the new.
Golden child.
Beautifully styled.
These are the makings of You.

I gotta protect my energy
* *Digga D*

I had a purpose before anyone had an opinion.
* *Jalen Hurts*

Healing

Healing begins where denial ends
through the intersection that is accountability.
Oftentimes it is what we are holding onto which is causing us the
most pain.
A tug of war with myself in the middle
my limbs the ropes being dragged in different directions.
                                       release the
tensions.

Free your inhibitions.

It's often in the luminescent soul we find peace. The absence of
heat, anger, and frustration, allows the rumination of rediscovering
ourselves. It ebbs and flows across the exoskeleton sending cooling
waves of prayer and power into our spirits.

To heal is to do deal is to feel
is to appeal to the surreal
not conceal what is real.

Youth is happy because it has the capacity to beauty. Anyone who keeps the ability to see beauty never grows old.
* Franz Kafka

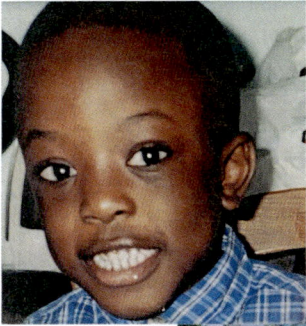

A letter to my younger self

Man, don't ever doubt yourself.
An unconventional journey of ups and downs.
Say what you truly feel.
Empathy is your greatest strength but it's also your kryptonite.

Owning your past is seldom easy.
Keep true to the kid who dreamed so big.
Once a child with the world on his fingertips,
now grown with the weight of it on your shoulders.
Relax, rejuvenate and release.

We cannot change what we are not aware of, and once we are aware, we cannot help but change.
* *Sheryl Sanberg*

God bless these 20-somethings.
* *SZA*

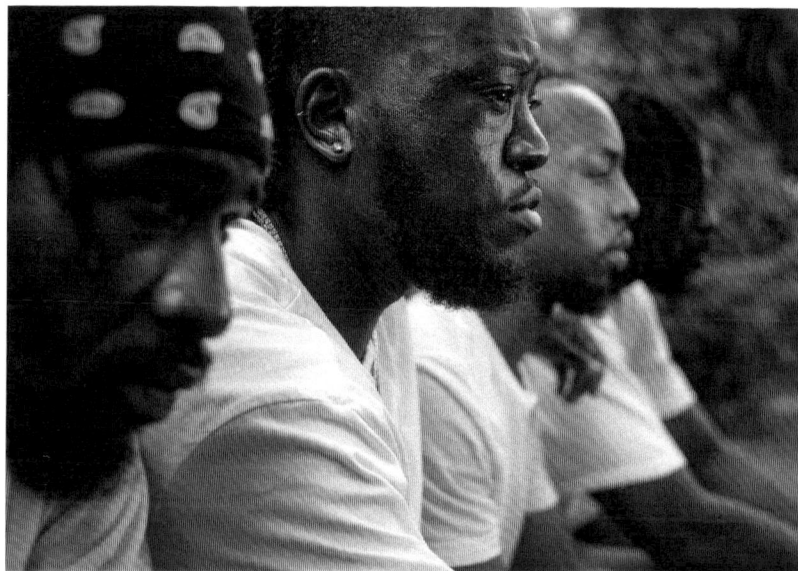

Pending

Pending the ending of an era.
Exiting what felt like forever and ever.
Neglecting what's causing disconnection.
Dejecting the feelings that are intersecting.
Investing in the now.
Never going back to what hurt you.
Go onward, go easy, go hard, stay true.

They tried to bury us. They didn't know we were the seeds.
    ✶ *Dinos Christianopoulos*

We delight in the beauty of the butterfly, but rarely admit the changes it has gone through to achieve that beauty.
    ✶ *Maya Angelou*

Perhaps the mission of an artist is to interpret beauty to people - the beauty within themselves.
    ✶ *Langston Hughes*

An ode to the Årchangelz

This is an ode to the Årchangelz,
the dark angels, from the dark ages to the coming-of-ages.

The enchanted ones, whose beauty is too abundant to fit into the narrow landscapes of westernised ideals.

Long before you were even conceived and after you've been perceived, you have always been worthy.
Your appeal is refined and pure. Celestial minds of divine understanding, keep your kindred spirits close, true camaraderie is a powerful beacon of solace.

God sculpted, crafted and chiselled you to perfection. We gaze at the translucent halo that gleams amongst your bronzed-skinned complexion.
Heavenly bodies, raw, cultivated. Iridescent in the moonlit sky. Your ethereal silver wings lift our smiles and our spirits up, and like fiery chariots you set our hearts ablaze.

Don't let deceitful demons of a duplicitous nature hiss in your ears. You are angelic. I pray you never forget it.
Above all you have a heart of gold. You are the epitome of what striving, and success looks like.
You see beauty in me because that beauty has always existed within you.

Emancipate yourselves from mental slavery. None but our-selves can free our minds. Have no fear for atomic energy 'cause none of them can stop the time.

✳ Bob Marley

For what's money without happiness?
Or hard times without the people you love
Though I'm not sure what's 'bout to happen next
I asked for strength from the Lord up above

✳ J. Cole

---

break free

Wealthy in the ways money cannot buy.
It is deeper than fast cars and looking fly. Cradled
by societal insecurities, b r e a k

                                 the

chains.

Step into the beauty of your character.
Reach out from the nest. Spread your wings.
Do not limit yourself to materialistic things.
Only you can f r e e yourself and fly from the

birdcage
of
your
repression.

If I fail, If I succeed at least, I'd live as I believed.
   ✳ Whitney Houston

*If I didn't define myself for myself, I would be crunched into
other people's fantasies for me and eaten alive.*
   ✳ Audre Lorde

The Kaleidoscope of Nubian Dreams

Why is it so hard to define?
It's a spectrum of many sides but where do we align? We're put into these boxes and labelled like products, fetishised for our bodies, demoralised when we show emotion, criminalised when we speak up and dehumanised when we want to live our human lives.

Sweet like chocolate but we're the ones left with the bitter after taste.

From the Mandem to dem man there. Those guys on the block stop and stare.
But what if we embraced our brothers, loved one another, the untapped potential we'd discover if we didn't tear down each other.

Been this way from day 1 to infinity, matter of fact it's my masculinity.

My masculinity masks the ills you throw at me. It masks the stark, suicidal thoughts in the dark. It embarks through self-doubt. It has no feet but it's always about.

My masculinity hated himself, it berated himself, it cremated himself. Until enough was enough. Ashes to ashes, dust to dust, no more self-hate. They're gonna have to learn how to adjust.

My masculinity is the chorus of a J Hus tune. It's the warmth at the end of June but it's cold like our fits when the Mandem roll through. It blooms at 21 like so solid crew.

My masculinity is limitless. It's gentle it takes care of U and I like business. It leads with love pumping from the heart, its art; it's been that way from the start.

My masculinity is golden. It's lavish, it's sexy, it got drip, it's got grills and vvs' it's all the beauty that it possesses. Word to Whitney.

Black women are the blueprint. What's masculinity without its divine counterpart, the heart, the heartbeat the rhythms, the fabric the fine linens which keeps the world spinning and spinning in style.

Unravelling and unveiling the brightest minds, entertainers, athletes, engineers, models, teachers and visionaries. Come through the motherland like missionaries. Seasoned like Salt-N-Pepa it's very necessary.

All excellent black boys derive from the black Madonna. Tenderness pours into our souls and out through our ample lips. It drips through our mother tongue; style and swagger.

It's in our twists, locs and waves, shea butter, honey and pomade. It's in the image that God made.

It transcends the perceptions of the short-sighted white male gaze. It's a spectrum. A kaleidoscope of Nubian dreams. My masculinity feels the blues, gets the green and sees the gold.

We are not monolithic, we are polylithic, prolific, terrific, non-specific, no gimmicks. You wouldn't understand it like hieroglyphics. We know our roots run deep like the Nile, like I said you wouldn't understand it. They tried to reprimand it, we bare witness first handed, but now they demand it, command it and yet still misunderstand it.

For it only needs my validity, it's my masculinity.

VII. CATHARSIS

noun /kəˈθɑːsɪs/

The process of releasing, and
thereby providing relief from,
strong or repressed emotions.

———————

*Everything has changed and yet, I am more me
than I've ever been.*
✻ Iain Thomas

*'For I know the plans I have for you,' declares the LORD,
'plans to prosper you and not to harm you, plans to give
you hope and a future.'*
✻ Jeremiah 29;11

———————

JÅNUS pt. 2

Processing
    Precious
        Poignant
      Evocative
    Freeing
   T r a n s c i e n t being
We face each other head-to-head, eye-to-eye, heart-to-heart. The making of me. The yin to my yang.

You are my peace, my war, an idyllic picturesque village that lives in my heart. A barren wasteland resides in my mind, wrapped in barbed wire and jagged unsaid thoughts.

Our collision created the cosmic gateway to my new beginning. Pigments of phthalo green, rebirth, a breast of land providing growth and nutrients. It flows into visions of indigo; a collection of memories joyful and poignant cascades into a psychedelic pool of magenta; a swirling aroma of euphoric culture swimming in the air.

This culminates in an amalgam of a rapid TV static:

First loves. Resentment. School trips. Scrapped knees. Summer. Infatuation. Hospital. Birthdays. Video games. MSN. BBM. Bubble language. Kickers. PS2. DLR. Morley's. Fresh trims. Tears. Notting Hill Carnival. Air Max 95s. Shoreditch. Brick Lane Market. Barbershop. Uni accommodation. 9-5. Raves. Graduation. Stage lights. Long nights. Flights.

Life.

t r a n s e n d e n t clarity.

Darkness is only the external absence of light, not its antithesis. The light comes from within, its internal luminous glow highlights the beauty of our being.

Endings are the start of a new beginning.

Acknowledgements

It truly takes a village of supporting and loving people for this to all be possible.

Firstly, I would like to thank God. I'm forever grateful for your grace and blessings upon my life.

My family, my mother and father and my two older brothers. Thank you for your love, sacrifice, immense level of patience and support throughout my life and through this book. There aren't enough words in the world to express what you mean to me.

To my grandparents, aunties, uncles and cousins, thank you for nurturing, caring and loving me. I'm genuinely very blessed to have each and every one of you.

Femmesocial Press, thank you for your support and giving me a platform to express my work.

Petra, this would not even be fathomable without you. Thank you for encouraging, supporting, publishing, editing and most importantly believing in me.

Thank you, Lou Smith, for your brilliant photography, the images capture my vision vividly and I'm grateful for your dedication and artistry.

Vendula and Ema, thank you so much for bringing my artistic vision to life through your graphic designs.

Wale Show and the Maktub community, thank you for creating a safe space that nurtures actors and creatives. I have met some of the most talented artists and attended workshops have truly helped me to hone my craft. Thank you for giving me a diverse and engaging platform to express my words.

Alex thank you for your support and authenticity.

Levi thank you for your constant encouragement and infectious positivity.

Dorcas thank you for being such a bright light in my life, your support is very appreciated.

Dejean thank you for your love, support and encouragement.

Patrie thank you for your selfless support and devotion to your craft.
Matt thank you for encouraging me when I felt lost in all this.
James Amatruda and James Pele, my Bathway Boyz, thank you guys for supporting me, I'm very proud of our teamwork and our camaraderie enforced through hard work and brilliant results.
Oonagh, India, Chelsea, Maya, Niamh, Tilly, Georgie and Valbona thank you for all your talent, care and support.
Bettina, my unsung hero thank you so much for always reaching out to me and supporting.
Tobore, thank you for all your guidance, love and support.
Okeam Briscoe, thank you so much for your support, talent and friendship, thank you for being a genuine and vulnerable soul.
Anita thank you for your efficiency, liveliness and diligence you are truly inspiring.
Zina and Chloe thank you so much for your kindness, love and support.
Panashe, thank you so much for your support, friendship and care.
Godwin, Marty and Will thank you for your selfless support, talent and care.
Dr John Morton, thank you for being the spark which made me even consider writing my own poetry.
Dr Harry Derbyshire, Dr Justine Baillie, Jillian Wallis, Dr Simon Bowes, Dr Natasha Oxley, Dr Nick Holden, Dr James McLaughlin, Dr David Hockham and Ed Currie. My brilliant lecturers and university staff, thank you for your unwavering support.
Sarah Mole, Melissa Whitington, Sarah Stoneham, Jacqui Webster. Thank you for teaching, supporting, showing up for me and genuinely caring for me.
Thank you Amber Claydon, Veronica Clarke and Imogen Edmundson for being the reason I fell in love with performance and theatre, thank you for impacting a young quiet black boy with such knowledge and encouragement.
Mary Brack. Thank you for your encouragement and helping me to recognise the abilities that I didn't know I possessed.
I would like to thank all those who love me that I am yet to meet.

Lastly, to all the incredible game changers, trailblazers, visionaries that have come before me and opened doors for me. I am eternally grateful for your vulnerability, talent and perseverance.

Resources:

I realise that many of the poems written cover deeply triggering topics and issues. Below I have decided to provide resources to help anyone who is currently struggling. If any of the words have triggered unresolved feelings know you matter, you are important and you are more loved than you will ever know.

Mental health:

The S.M.I.L.E-ing Boys Project is a happiness research-based programme created by Kai Rufai. Through using poetry, photography film and podcasts they support mental health and challenge negative stereotypes. Their goal is to provide a positive narrative to empower black boys to express their emotions and experiences. *https://universoulartist.com/smiling-boys-project/*

• **Black Minds Matter UK:** Connects Black individuals and families with free mental health services — by professional Black therapists. Visit *blackmindsmatteruk.com*
• **The Black, African and Asian Therapy Network (BAATN):** The UK's largest independent organisation to specialise in working psychologically with Black, African, South Asian and Caribbean people. Visit *baatn.org.uk*

Online Resources and Information
• **Young Minds:** Provides information and advice for young people, including resources specific to Black mental health. Visit *youngminds.org.uk* and search for their resources on race and mental health.
• **Mind's Black, Asian, and Minority Ethnic (BAME) Resources:** Offers information on mental health issues specifically affecting BAME communities. Visit *mind.org.uk* and search for BAME resources.

Support Groups and Communities
• **Therapy for Black Girls UK:** Aims to make mental health topics more relevant and accessible for Black women and girls. Visit *therapyforblackgirls.com*
• **Nilaari:** A Black, Asian and Minority Ethnic led charity delivering culturally appropriate and accessible talking therapies and social support. Visit *nilaari.co.uk*

Professional Help
• **Black Thrive:** Aims to improve the mental health and wellbeing of Black communities in Lambeth. Visit *blackthrive.org.uk*

Mental Health Resources in the UK:

Your mental health is important. If you or someone you know is struggling, there are many resources available to provide support. Below is a list of organisations and services that can help.

Emergency Contacts:
- **Samaritans:** Available 24/7 for anyone who needs to talk. Call 116 123 or visit *samaritans.org*
- **NHS Urgent Mental Health Helpline:** For urgent support, contact your local NHS helpline. Visit *nhs.uk/service-search/mental-health/find-an-urgent-mentalhealth-helpline* for more details.

Helplines and Support Services:
- **Mind:** Offers advice and support to empower anyone experiencing a mental health problem. Call 0300 123 3393 or visit *mind.org.uk*
- **Shout Crisis Text Line:** Free, confidential, 24/7 text messaging support service. Text "SHOUT" to 85258 or visit *giveusashout.org*

Online Resources and Information:
- **NHS Every Mind Matters:** Tips and advice for mental health. Visit *nhs.uk/every-mindmatters*
- **Mental Health Foundation:** Provides a wide range of information on mental health topics. Visit *mentalhealth.org.uk*

Professional Help:
- **Your GP:** Speak to your GP about any mental health concerns for advice and potential referrals.
- **BACP (British Association for Counselling and Psychotherapy):** Find a certified therapist near you. Visit *bacp.co.uk*

Support Groups and Communities:
- **Rethink Mental Illness:** Provides support groups and services. Call 0808 801 0525 or visit *rethink.org*
- **Anxiety UK:** Offers support for those living with anxiety. Call 03444 775 774 or visit *anxietyuk.org.uk*

Sexual Assault:

If you or someone you know has experienced sexual assault, there are many resources available in the UK to offer support, guidance, and assistance. Below is a list of organisations and services dedicated to helping survivors of sexual assault.

Emergency Contacts:
- **Police:** In an emergency, dial 999 for immediate assistance.
- **NHS:** For urgent medical care, visit your nearest A&E (Accident & Emergency) department or call 111 for advice. Helplines and Support Services
- **Rape Crisis England & Wales:** Offers confidential support and information for women and girls who have experienced sexual violence. Call 0808 802 9999 or visit *rapecrisis.org.uk*

Online Resources and Information:
- **The Survivors Trust:** Provides support for all survivors of rape and sexual abuse. Call 08088 010 818 or visit *thesurvivorstrust.org*
- **Samaritans:** Provides emotional support for anyone in distress. Call 116 123 or visit *samaritans.org*

Helplines and Support Services:
- **SurvivorsUK:** Supports men, boys, and non-binary people who have been affected by sexual violence. Visit *survivorsuk.org*
- **Victim Support:** Offers free and confidential help to victims of crime, including sexual assault. Call 08 08 16 89 111 or visit *victimsupport.org.uk*
- **Refuge:** Provides support for women and children experiencing domestic violence, including sexual assault. Call 0808 2000 247 or visit *refuge.org.uk*

Support Groups and Communities
- **Women and Girls Network (WGN):** Provides free, confidential services for women and girls who have experienced gendered violence. Visit *wgn.org.uk*

Professional Help:
• **NHS Sexual Assault Referral Centres (SARCs):** Provide medical, practical, and emotional support. Visit *nhs.uk* to find a SARC near you.
• **British Association for Counselling and Psychotherapy (BACP):** Find a qualified therapist who specialises in sexual trauma. Visit *bacp.co.uk*

Discrimination:

Discrimination can take many forms and affect individuals in various ways. If you or someone you know is experiencing discrimination, there are resources available in the UK to provide support. Below is a list of services and organisations dedicated to helping those facing discrimination.

Online Resources and Information:
• **Equality and Human Rights Commission (EHRC):** Provides information and guidance on discrimination laws and individual rights. Visit *equalityhumanrights.com*
• **Gov.uk Discrimination Page:** Offers information on discrimination and legal rights in the UK. Visit *gov.uk/discrimination-your-rights*
• **Stop Hate UK:** Provides support for individuals affected by hate crime and discrimination. Call 0800 138 1625 or visit *stophateuk.org*

Support Groups and Communities:
• **Race Equality Foundation:** Works to promote race equality in social support and public services. Visit *raceequalityfoundation.org.uk*
• **Stonewall:** Supports LGBTQ+ individuals facing discrimination and works towards equality. Call 08000 50 20 20 or visit *stonewall.org.uk*
• **Disability Rights UK:** Provides support and advocacy for people with disabilities facing discrimination. Call 0330 995 0400 or visit *disabilityrightsuk.org*

Professional Help:
• **Law Centres Network:** Provides free legal advice and representation to those facing discrimination. Visit *lawcentres.org.uk*
• **British Association for Counselling and Psychotherapy (BACP):** Find a therapist who specialises in issues related to discrimination. Visit *bacp.co.uk*